# 31
# FAVORED
# DECISIONS

Dr. Jerry A. Grillo, Jr

**31 Favored Decisions**

Copyright 2020 By Jerry A. Grillo, Jr.

FZM PUBLISHING
P.O. Box 3707
Hickory, NC. 28603

# Table of Contents:

# AUTHOR'S COMMENTS

It is my deepest hope that this book brings health and healing to every area of your life. My aim is to expand your understanding so you can increase in wisdom.

Your life matters to me!

I have spent the better part of my life writing, preaching, teaching, and traveling; however, these moments are never taken lightly. At the age of eighteen, when God called me, He equipped me to help you win. For this I am honored.

I pray this book, "31 Favored Decisions," enables you to make better decisions. Remember, "if one bad decision can bring you into a bad place, then, one right decision can get you out."

I pray, daily, God will enable you to walk in the FOG (Favor of God).

Love you,
Dr. G

# INTRODUCTION

Every good, or bad, situation in life started with a decision. Many of which have been shaping our lives since we were children. Every moment entered, and exited, was the result of a decision. And, with every decision, the need for wisdom increases which promotes greater success. Studying is necessary for understanding how to excel in our jobs, our relationships, our finances, etc. However, increase hinges on the power of a decision. No one can increase without favor. If you could change your past, how many decisions would you alter? My wife gets frustrated when I hesitate in making decisions; vacillating has always been one of my biggest problems. Why? Because I fear the consequences of wrong decisions. Fear is a disabling force preventing people from making timely decisions.

Once a decision is made, it is important to establish focus then point people in that direction. In confidence, move forward, knowing you are moving in the right direction while understanding there could be a better way in the future. Decisions are not permanent; however, they are thoughts that can lead to additional information.

It is also necessary to trust yourself when making decisions. And, to have success, deciding swiftly, and decisively, is a very important skill to have. This is not theory, but fact.

Imagine a world where lines are all you see. And, imagine those lines represent frequencies connected to the line above it, and the one below it. Think about this, every cell phone is a frequency. Through dialing a certain set of numbers, I am able to connect to any cell phone throughout the world. Like cell phones, people operate on a frequency as well; it is called the law of vibrations. **Thoughts have energy,** and according to Thomas Edison, *"Thoughts are things."* Many times, I have been overwhelmed by wrong thoughts, they have taken over my mind and my day.

## CASTING DOWN

*"casting down arguments and every high thing that exalts itself against the knowledge of God, bringing every thought into captivity to the obedience of Christ, and being ready to punish all disobedience when your obedience is fulfilled"* (2 Cor 10:5,6)

This scripture implies, I have to make up my mind and force my thoughts to go elsewhere. The imaginations of the mind can be overwhelming. It is only through quality decisions that those thoughts can be forcefully removed and, then, replaced with new thoughts that bring renewal.

Decisions are energy converted into frequencies which make a demand on the ether around you. Have you ever been thinking about someone then, suddenly, that person calls? In this instance, a frequency was released enabling the other person to connect which, then, prompted the phone call. Because thoughts are more powerful than a laser beam, the obsessive thoughts of yesterday could be today's reality. By changing how we think, we can elevate our lives to a higher level of living. Do you spend your time thinking about the bad things that have happened in your life? If so, you are, most likely, stuck in a wound. Do you spend time thinking, or worrying, about tomorrow?

Then, you are probably stuck in a fantasy. In order to be set free, it is important to retrain your mind to live in the here, and now. By deciding to let go of the past, tomorrow can take care of itself.

## DECISIONS CAN HEAL

It is surprising how a person views life as well as the world around him. The mind is an amazing tool that enables you to take control of every situation. Though things can, and do, happen
outside of our control, the decisions we make can determine the outcome. An incredible euphoria takes place when you realize a victory after having harnessed the power of a smart decision.

## DECISION GUIDELINES

- Make up your mind
- Decide what you want
- Take action
- Monitor what works as well and what doesn't
- Don't be afraid to adjust
- Remember, you are in control. Changing your mind, or your strategies, is not wrong.

## FACTS ABOUT DECISIONS

- Stay committed
- Be willing to change
- Enjoy making decisions
- Take a chance

- Risk is the seed for great rewards.

# 1

# THE ACCESS
# YOU DECIDE TO PURSUE

*Access is very important and is the proof of favor.*

When someone makes the decision to favor you, access to that person is also given. Because the information gleaned through right connection can be priceless, it is as powerful as money. And, when their knowledge is correctly applied, it can immensely change lives. Access doesn't happen on its own, it must be pursued. Giving up your time, your money, as well as some conveniences are necessary in order to be in a position to acquire access to the right people.

*The right access can accelerate your success rate.*

There is right access as well as wrong access. If right access can accelerate success, then, wrong access can have the opposite effect by accelerating failure. It is important to know the person being pursued for access; the goal is to become like the one who succeeds, not fails. So, look for the person who is at a higher level of success, or who is in a greater season of prosperity. Then, determine to ask, receive, and apply their secrets of success. Always be

13

ready to give audience to a mentor instead of the other way around.

***Access has to be pursued.***

Those unwilling to pursue access disqualifies the individual from receiving.

***Access is as valuable as money.***

Welfare is defined as one who sits, and waits, for a handout; it is favor without action. Welfare is an entitlement mentality, ***the attitude that someone owes you.*** However, the truth is, no one owes anyone anything. This mentality can, and will, destroy companies, churches, relationships, and governments. Do you desire to win? Is living life beyond the boundaries of mediocrity your hope? Have you come to the end of yesterday's decisions? Pursue access! Find somebody worth pursuing then, serve them…honor them…and, respect them. In doing this, they will have the confidence to reveal their personal journey of success. **Pursuing access is a major decision that should not be taken lightly.** A mentor can offer methods of success, often times, eliminating the pain that comes with trial and error.

***Access provides information that would otherwise be off limits.***

It is possible to gain higher levels of wisdom by having access to individuals who know more than you or have achieved more. Some time back, During an INSP Television Telethon, I had the opportunity to serve Dr.

Mike Murdock. During that time, he received a call from a Movie Producer/Millionaire requesting a visit. Out of respect, I offered to leave, however, Dr. Mike asked that I stay; he wanted to introduce me to his guest. After "listening" to these giants of God, for over two-hours, I gained information and ideas that came as a result of having access to Dr. Mike Murdock. Their wisdom will always be an indispensable asset.

***Access allows you to enter areas you've only dreamed about.***

Without access, being stuck is the only available option; so, never underestimate the power of access. Protect the favor you have and, be respectful. Do not allow anyone to enter the environment who would jeopardize a mentor's freedom to speak. I learned this unpleasant lesson when mine visited the Favor Life Church. His whole attitude was different, he was frustrated, and he seemed to want to end our conversations very quickly. Privately, due to sensing his irritability, I asked what I had done wrong. His answer was, "I AM." "You continue to allow people to come into my presence without my permission; I gave access to you, not the whole church. This has trivialized our relationship and has made it common." Because it has been my personality to allow everyone access, I was horrified. However, through that experience, I quickly learned the value of treasuring, and honoring, the access extended to me. Respect is key! When others are in the room, do not enter a mentor's presence without permission. And, do not bring uninvited individuals. Through honoring access, invitations can be granted to amazing conferences full of powerful messages. Being granted access to certain

individuals can also open doors to other gifted leaders –
this is favor!

# 2

# THE FRIENDSHIP
# YOU DECIDE TO KEEP

◆———————————————————◆

*Not everyone around you belongs around you.*

*"Those who cannot discern your worth and value disqualify for your friendship."*

I have learned, the hard way, that cutting off people from a current season, in order to enter the next, is never easy. With my personality, and how I love surrounding myself with people, this is especially difficult. However, experience has suggested, the majority of those individuals won't qualify to stay connected. And, it can be very dangerous to carry friends into the next season. In the life of success, it is important to understand that not everyone truly stands in your vision, nor is everyone against it.

There are people who are full of incredible potential, however, they can never get out of their present season. The reason they are stuck is due, in part, from their resistance in separating from a current friendship stream. As a result, they can never really get ahead and, many times, they find themselves back where they started. Instead of holding on to stagnant friendships, look for new and thriving mentors who can equip for the next season.

## A Decision Will Qualify You for Favor

- Who can I trust with access?
- Can I trust them to hear my conversations with others?
- Who can I trust to participate in my private life?
- Can I trust them with my personal experiences?
- Who can I trust to see me vulnerable?

Anyone you call friend must be able to separate the friendship from the Mantle. If this is not possible, or refused, don't allow access. Access is a trusted position preventing what is private from being revealed to an enemy. It is important to know that not everyone is trust worthy; they don't have the character to protect their mentor's privacy.

**Let me caution you!** Not everyone serves out of respect, they are enemies waiting to expose a weakness in order to destroy what has been built. Qualify everyone! It is sometimes important to do background checks to determine if those desiring to serve will be a partner, or a predator.

## People You Are Unable to Mentor

- Those who think you are their problem
- Those who do not value what you deem important
- Those who refuse mentorship
- Those who ignore instructions

- Those who weaken your faith
- Those who hate what you love
- Those who are comfortable sitting at your enemy's table
- Those who do not defend you in your absence
- Those who refuse to support your financial vision
- Those who believe they know more than you
- Those who get jealous over your blessings
- Those who refuse to honor you with gifts
- Those who see you as their friend, or family
- Those who will not recognize the gifts God has placed in you
- Those who cannot take correction
- Those who refuse to tithe
- Those who refuse to change
- Those who are unwilling to admit they need you
- Those who are comfortable in the presence of the ungodly
- Those who are willing to expose your weakness

I would have saved myself years of heartache, and grief, if I could have had access to this, powerful, list.

So, stop trying to win the world, give access to those you have been assigned and begin helping them to change.

# 31 Favored Decisions

# 3

# THE DREAM
# YOU DECIDE TO MAKE
# YOUR OBSESSION

◆――――――――――――――――――◆

The more dreams you have, the harder it is to stay focused. So, it is important to narrow them down until your energy is focused, rather than divided. Someone once asked, "How do you kill a visionary?" The answer was to give him more than one dream.

*A dream is a fanciful vision of the conscious mind; a fond hope or aspiration, images of thoughts passing through the psyche.*

A dream is the power to leave your present place and enter a world that is not controlled by your fears and doubts. You see, when you dream, the sky is the limit. I've often said, "If you are going to dream, leave your check book at home." What dream have you made an obsession? Worse yet, what dream have you tabled, or shelved, because someone told you it was impossible? Many times, I have stared into hollow eyes because life's circumstances caused an abortion of their dreams; dreams that began early in their youth. A failed marriage, a wayward child, a late mortgage payment, a car repossessed, or any number of things could sideline a person's dreams. Instead of pushing through, there was an acceptance, and a settling, which prevented the pursuit of that dream. Don't stop dreaming! Without a dream, life would be void, hollow and empty. I can't imagine a life without dreaming.

- A dream is the only way to exit your crisis even for a, brief, moment.
- A dream is the only way to visit another place, or time.
- A dream is the only world where you don't need money or an education to succeed.

A famous line in the movie, **"THE FIELD OF DREAMS,"** said, "If you build it, they will come." I'm saying, "If you dream it, and believe it, you can achieve it." Your mind is your personal world; it is the place where dreams live. To keep those dreams alive requires discipline and a constant rehearsing of those dreams. This obsession eventually creates a path that enables the fulfillment of the ideas you have already been meditating. Your mind created a future photograph that became your present reality.

## Keys to Unlocking Your Favored Dream

- Decide what you want and, constantly, rehearse it.
- Decide which dream to focus on. How do you stop the success of a dreamer? By giving them too many dreams.
- Be the creator, you are the inspiration to pursue the dream.
- Search for the right mentor to communicate your

dreams, not everyone qualifies to hear them.
- Invest time, money, and focus into your dream.
- Build a picture, or dream wall.
- Never stop believing.
- Never stop dreaming.

In my book, "Live Big, Dream Big, Be Big," I have a whole chapter on the dream.

# 31 Favored Decisions

# 4

# THE ATMOSPHERE
# YOU DECIDE
# TO CREATE

◆————————————————————————◆

The atmosphere you create can promote a sense of focus. And, when I think of atmosphere, I think of the Wisdom Center. When I walk through the Wisdom Center, I begin to dream. And, as I do, excitement and anticipation create an expectancy for my future; for all that can be accomplished as a result of the dream.

Dr. Murdock, in my opinion, has mastered the art of creating an atmosphere conducive to success, and wisdom. He has a place he calls the "Writer's World," as well as a wall he calls his "Dream Wall." He has created an atmosphere that promotes fine tuning, or a greater focus, which brings about the productivity necessary for the dream's fulfillment.

*Atmosphere is defined as "a pervading or surrounding influence or spirit; general mood or social environment." It is "an interesting, often exotic, effect produced by decoration, furnishings, etc."*

Atmosphere matters, it is important for success. That being said, certain colors can cause different responses in people. So, be meticulous: paint the walls, hang pictures, pick pleasing furniture, etc. Ask yourself, "Does the atmosphere provide the stimulation necessary for me to win?"

# Remember:

- Atmosphere creates mood.
- Atmosphere produces good, or bad, reactions.
- Atmosphere determines the seed sown.
- Atmosphere creates focus.

Set out to create an atmosphere that brings comfort and peace to your surroundings. Look at your office…study your house in order to determine its level of peace and comfort. Don't wait, start today! For me, changing the atmosphere often includes filling the room with the type of music that will help to stimulate my creativity. This helps me to write longer, and better.

If your desire is to have more romance in your marriage, then set the mood; light some candles, place flowers around the room, and put on some soft music. Atmosphere can make all the difference. Personally, I've experienced increased motivation, and greater victories, simply by changing my atmosphere.

*Allowing the wrong people into your presence can destroy your confidence.*

Avoid negative people. Negativity can destroy the

excitement you have for the project at hand. Always silence the voices which are speaking against what you are working to accomplish.

***Do you want to know or be closer to God?*** Create an atmosphere of worship. I love walking in a room where worship music has been playing. As a matter of fact, I keep worship music playing in my green room as well as the Favor Life sanctuary. I believe the enemy avoids the room where worship is offered on a constant basis. Many times, I have walked through these rooms and experienced the presence of the Holy Spirit and,
immediately, tears would come to my eyes.

***Worship creates an atmosphere where God is present...***

***It's obvious that God is into atmosphere.*** God created a whole choir of Angels who would sing, "Holy, Holy, Holy is the Lord God Almighty." This tells us He is attracted to the atmosphere of praise; He inhabits the praises of His people. (Psalm 22:3) Before the tabernacle was built, God gave instructions on how it should be built, how it should smell, and how the lighting should be. If the Almighty takes delight in the right atmosphere, I believe, as people made in His image and likeness, we should also.

# 5

# THE AUTHORITY
# YOU DECIDE TO WALK IN

*"Submit yourselves for the Lord's sake to every authority instituted among men: whether to the king, as the supreme authority..."* (1 Peter 2:13-14 NIV)

There is a big difference between **power,** and **authority**; you may have the power to do something but not the authority. Which is greater, power or authority? Authority carries more weight than power. For instance, a Police Officer does not possess the strength to stop a speeding vehicle. However, the authority afforded him, through the badge he carries, prompts a person to pull his car off the road upon seeing the officer's blue lights. His badge carries State and Federal authority.

*"I have given you authority to trample on snakes and scorpions and to overcome all the power of the enemy; nothing will harm you."* (Luke 10:19-20 NIV)

***Authority is force, capability, competency, freedom, mastery, delegated influence...***

God has provided us with not only power but authority.

We lack the natural power to withstand, or oppose, sickness, failure, pain, and attacks. However, we have the authority to flash our spiritual badges and confess the name of Jesus in order to receive the power necessary to overcome those obstacles. All authority was given to Jesus and He, in turn, has given it to His people. So, why do we, as Christians, seem to be tossed like leaves in the wind?

One reason, we lack the understanding of that authority. Our position, in Christ, makes us more than conquerors. But, in our natural condition, we have no power. What does it mean to be more than a conqueror? Years ago, a boxer named, Evander Holyfield, won a heavy weight match. After the fight, he was standing in the ring with swollen eyes, bleeding lips, and an aching body. He was holding a check for millions of dollars which he preceded to hand to his, beautiful, wife. When the millions passed from his hand, to hers, she became more than a conqueror. This is exactly what Jesus has done for us. He fought the fight, died on the cross, and rose from the dead. After Jesus won, God handed His Son the Crown, then He placed it on His bride (the church). By crowning the church, we became more! More than a conqueror.

Make today the day you take back all the enemy has stolen.

# 6

# THE ANGER
# YOU DECIDE TO CONTROL

---

*"How much more grievous are the consequences of anger than the causes of it." Marcus Aurelius*

*"Anything that begins in anger ends in shame..."*
*Benjamin Franklin*

- Anger is the strongest vice life can hold over us.
- Anger clouds your judgment.
- Out of control anger builds false imaginations and creates false enemies.

Anger can overpower the mind, therefore, those who make us angry can control us. It is important to understand that anger has a voice. And, when we give anger room to speak, it means we have stopped listening to the right voices. I know someone who has been saved, for many years, who reacts in the wrong way when angered. He allows that anger to control his mind, his decisions, and his relationships. He is controlled by anger rather than walking in the power of freedom.

*"Be ye angry, and sin not: let not the sun go down upon your wrath."* (Eph 4:26 KJV)

Let me be clear, you will never be able to live a life void of anger. People will always be exposed to someone angry, or, they themselves might be prone to having angry outbursts. At some point, people will disappoint you and cause you to be, or feel, angry. The bible gives us clear guidelines on how to keep anger from becoming an uncontrollable monster.

*First, get angry but sin not!* Don't allow anger to dictate how far, in the past, to take the battle; stick to the main cause. Otherwise, your mind will begin building false imaginations causing you to focus on other perceived injuries.

*Second, you have a 12-hour window.* Don't go to bed angry. Going to bed with an angry frame of mind opens the door to the spirit of anger. And, you are more likely to wake up angry. So, determine to get rid of all anger before bed; it will protect your heart from the root of anger.

**Facts About Anger:**

1. Anger is deadly.
2. Anger can ruin marriages and relationships.
3. Anger can destroy your future.
4. Anger can stop the blessings of God.

*"Do everything necessary to stop anger, otherwise, it will stop you." Jerry A. Grillo,*

# 7

# THE ATTITUDE YOU DECIDE TO EXERCISE

*You cannot dream yourself into a character; you must hammer and forge yourself one."*
*James A Froude*

*Attitude is character exposed.*

Attitude is a manner of acting that shows one's mental disposition.

*Without the proper attitude you will never achieve the success, or reach the potential, that God has always intended for you.*

*Attitude is as important as physical hygiene.*

As a matter of fact, your attitude is your spiritual hygiene. When your attitude stinks, it has the same effect as a person whose physical hygiene has been neglected. A bad attitude is repulsive! Unfortunately, opinions and judgments are made based upon a person's attitude, good or bad. So, don't allow sour or negative attitudes to build a stink around you.

***Attitude is posture revealed.***

How you talk... How you enter a room... your facial expressions... how you answer the telephone... all reveal your attitude!

***"Wars may be fought with weapons, but they are won by men. It is the spirit (attitude) of the men who follow and of the man who leads that gain the victory"*** George Patton, Jr.

***If you can't win the race, push the one ahead of you to break the record.***

Your attitude can determine whether, or not, you succeed. Attitudes are observed by others and can reveal feelings otherwise hidden. Most people never realize the power within them to change an attitude; it is the power to make things better.

What is an attitude?

- Attitude is the behavior, or mood, created by the thing we have determined to focus upon. It is a viewpoint, a state of mind.
- It is the force that determines whether you are favored. It has the power to multiply your efforts. It will attract, or repel, people, bosses, or leaders around you.
- Attitude is not a feeling but is birthed by a decision.

- When you decide to change your attitude, you have decided to change the world around you.
- Attitude is nothing more than the harvest of seed sown in your mind.
- Your attitude is affecting every relationship. It determines how a relationship will begin, or end.
- Your attitude can keep your mate from coming home.
- Remember, the goodness, and power, of God will help you maintain a right attitude.

## How to Maintain Your Attitude

- Mediate on good things... I like to mediate on God's word. "Thy word have I hid in my heart that I might not sin..." Psalm 119:11
- Surround your life with right sounds and silence the noise of negativity. Find music that lifts you into the ether of creativity.
- Pursue goals and dreams that promote the goodness of your future. Find worthwhile thoughts and force your mind to stay there.
- Insist on protecting every good thing you hear. What enters your mind will create a right attitude, or a wrong one.

Remember, when you make the decision to change your attitude, you can change your world.

# 31 Favored Decisions

# 8

# THE ADVICE YOU
# DECIDE TO FOLLOW

*"They that won't be counseled can't be helped."*

*"Wise men don't need advice. Fools won't take it."*
**Benjamin Franklin**

Advice simply means counsel. Whose counsel will you believe? Whose voice will you listen to? Along with counsel, a person's future is determined by the voice he has decided to believe.

**Who is talking to you?** No, better yet, whose counsel are you listening to?

I have witnessed many people, especially young adults, make major decisions that turned out to be wrong. Some of those, very costly, decisions included quitting jobs, dating people, marriage, and hanging out with the wrong people. These were major, life-changing, decisions that needed the advice of a mentor. However, in most cases, without any counsel, they jumped into a bad situation.

Every move of God is connected to His voice. He speaks

instructions into your life, then waits on you to follow through on what He spoke.

***The first counsel*** should always be the Holy Spirit. He has been given to guide, to comfort and, to lead the people of God.

***Second, you should*** wait for confirmation. God has anointed people like Pastors, Bishops, and Godly parents who can confirm what the Word of God.

***Third, there should*** be at least two or three witnesses to any, major, instruction.

Why are there so many divorces? In most cases, couples will not seek proper guidance, instead, they enter the marriage based on feelings. LOVE CAN WAIT, LUST CAN'T!

- Mentorship is important.
- Mentorship is the success without the wait.
- Mentorship is success without the struggle.

Mentorship is defined as the guidance provided by a mentor, especially an experienced person who can give the right advice for any, successful, endeavor. When guidance is given, it is not always what you want to hear. However, due to their expertise, it would be wise to listen.

Dr. Murdock once said, "My future is decided by the voice I choose to believe." That is strong! There have been several strong voices in my life including, in my early years, my dad's. When I was first saved, it was his voice that encouraged me to know my heavenly Father. As the second strong voice, Dr. Mike Murdock continues to unlock the potential that has always been within me.

Without strong guidance, you may never really discover your full potential. Many times, mentors see what you cannot. However, it is also necessary to qualify those who are giving advice. It is important that every word line up with the most powerful voice, The WORD OF GOD!

*Advice is sometimes hard to swallow.*

It is important to work on humility when taking advice.

*Remember, advice is not criticism.* If you interpret, and receive, advice as criticism you will immediately become defensive. This is why, I believe, married couples have a difficult time receiving guidance from their spouses.

Another definition for advice is counsel, assistance, and guidance. By allowing the right guidance into your life, it will help you make fewer mistakes.

# 31 Favored Decisions

# 9

# THE BITTERNESS YOU DECIDE TO LET HEAL

Bitterness is one of the most self-destructive poisons we can allow to stay in our lives. It is characterized by intense antagonism or hostility; it is resentful and cynical; it is anger and disappointment at being treated unfairly. Being bitter is like being bitten by a serpent whose poison slowly enters the bloodstream. Before you realize what's happening, bitterness corrupts everything it touches.

Bitterness is when disappointments, of the past, affect your present feelings and emotions in a negative way.

Bitterness is the grandson of anger and whose offspring is un-forgiveness. Bitterness appears 22 times in the KJV bible.

*Let all bitterness, wrath, anger, clamor, and evil speaking be put away from you, with all malice. 32 And be kind to one another, tenderhearted, forgiving one another, just as God in Christ forgave you.* (Eph 4:31-32 NKJV)

According to this scripture, it is clear that all bitterness must be removed. Therefore, those who call themselves

Christian must repent of all bitterness and all un-forgiveness.

*God didn't say He would take the bitterness from us.* He told us to put it off, then, be kind to one another, tenderhearted, forgiving one another; forgive even as God has forgiven us. We must do what He said and not allow our lives to be full of bitterness and unforgiveness.

*"looking diligently lest anyone fall short of the grace of God; lest any root of bitterness springing up cause trouble, and by this many become defiled;* (Heb 12:15-16 NKJV)

Where there is a root of bitterness, it may cause us to fall short of God's mercy and grace. A root grows far deeper than a season, or outburst, of anger; it goes to the core of our being. When bitterness finds a place to root, it will produce the fruit of bitterness which is contempt, hatred, animosity, etc.

Many have contaminated, or defiled, themselves because of the root of bitterness. Again, bitterness is like poison, when you are poisoned with its root, then those around you are subject to that same poison. The antidote for bitterness requires action on our part; it requires repentance! Otherwise, it corrupts all that it touches. Don't be dangerous, and useless, be forgiving instead. Let go of those who hurt you, and be a master healer of the hurting.

Those who are bitter, and full of anger, are hostage to a memory. Instead of staying trapped, work at becoming a hostage to your dreams! A Hateful and Bitter mind is a closed mind. You will never live a favored, or fulfilled, life while allowing bitterness to stay in your heart.

### *How to overcome the hurt created by bitterness?*

- Acknowledge the bitterness.
- Confess all bitterness.
- Refuse to conceal any bitterness.
- Release all bitterness.

# 31 Favored Decisions

# 10

## THE COVENANT YOU DECIDE TO KEEP

A covenant is a promise made between two parties. And, all of Christian power, and longevity, is based on a covenant. The bible is divided into two covenants, the Old, and the New Testament.

The word covenant appears 292 times in the King James Version. The first time the word was used, God was speaking to Noah and made a covenant between them.

*But with thee will I establish my covenant; and thou shalt come into the ark, thou, and thy sons, and thy wife, and thy sons' wives with thee.* (Gen 6:18 KJV)

When someone makes a covenant, it is a contract for life. Because we live in a country where contracts are easily broken, covenants are very hard to understand. A marriage covenant is to be for life, yet by going to court, that contract can be broken. Bankruptcy is another example of breaking contracts. However, in God's world, a covenant is a covenant; it is non-breakable.

The English definition of covenant means a binding and

solemn agreement to do, or keep from doing, a specified thing. It is an agreement among members of a church to defend and maintain its doctrines, policies, and faith.

When God decided to make a covenant with Abram, because He could swear by no one greater, He swore by Himself (Heb 6:13). In that day, for a covenant to be binding, two parties had to bring something to the meeting place. They had to walk between what was presented and swear, by their own name, they would stay in the contract. This was usually done by killing an animal and walking between the two halves. In the covenant between God and Abram, animals were brought, cut in half, and a flaming torch passed between the pieces while Abram fell into a deep sleep. Then, God swears by His own name and makes the promise to Abram.

*I will make my covenant between me and thee and will multiply thee exceedingly.* (Gen 17:2 KJV)

*I will establish my covenant between me and thee and thy seed after thee in their generations for an everlasting covenant, to be a God unto thee, and to thy seed after thee.* (Gen 17:7 KJV)

Be very careful about making covenants you can't keep. And, take your time when deciding to covenant with a church body. God does not allow those covenants to be broken as easily as we might assume. People could be living under a curse because of leaving a church body while under covenant with a Man of God. Being released by the one who watches over your soul is the proper way to leave. I encourage you to do the right thing.

***How you leave one season determines how you enter the next season.***

Marriage is a covenant between two people, so, let me close with this bit of advice. "Keep your eyes wide open before marriage and half shut afterwards."

# 31 Favored Decisions

# 11

## THE COURAGE YOU DECIDE TO SHOW

---

*"Courage, it would seem, is nothing less than the power to overcome danger, misfortune, fear, injustice, while continuing to affirm inwardly that life with all its sorrows is good; that everything is meaningful even if in a sense beyond our understanding; and that there is always tomorrow."*
*Dorothy Thompson*

**Be of good courage, and he shall strengthen your heart, all ye that hope in the LORD.** (Ps 31:24 KJV)

**Be strong and of a good courage: for unto this people shalt thou divide for an inheritance the land, which I swore unto their fathers to give them.7 Only be thou strong and very courageous, that thou may observe to do according to all the law, which Moses my servant commanded thee: turn not from it to the right hand or to the left, that thou may prosper whithersoever thou goest.** (Josh 1:6-7 KJV)

**Courage is the most valuable virtue you can have.**
If you plan on going against the norm, it's going to require

49

courage. If you plan on being different, it will require courage. If you've decided to be your own person instead of the person people want you to be, you will need courage.

Courage is the attitude of facing, and dealing, with anything recognized as dangerous, difficult or painful, instead of withdrawing from it. Courage is determination to face your past without being affected by it. This virtue is needed in order to move beyond the mediocrity of society as well as to unlock the excellence of the Kingdom.

Courage reveals itself when you can conclude that life is still good even after seeing all the hurt and pain; even after hearing all the bad things people have done. It is at its best when you are able to get up each day and face whatever comes your way without fear.

Courage is the ability of a mother to press on even after the loss of a child. It is the determination of a husband to carry on, and do what is required of him, after the loss of his spouse. It is when a child wakes up every morning knowing that peer pressure is waiting for him at school. It takes courage to face every one of these situations.

Courage is standing up for what is right in a world that loves doing wrong. It is a powerful tool that enables people to stand up and fight, without surrendering to the circumstances.

***Courage is uncommon valor.***

Be strong in courage today! Stand up and be counted!

Unlock and expand the Kingdom!

Remember the Lion who needed courage in the movie, 'Wizard of Oz?' It was stated, "If I only had courage…The lion would be King!"

## Conversation of the Cowardly

**Cowardly Lion:** All right, I'll go in there for Dorothy. Wicked Witch or no Wicked Witch, guards or no guards, I'll tear them apart. I may not come out alive, but I'm going in there. There's only one thing I want you fellows to do.

**Tin Man and Scarecrow:** What's that?

**Cowardly Lion: <u>Talk me out of it!</u>**

*Just before they meet the Wizard in the Emerald City the Cowardly Lion muses about what it would be like to be the king of the forest, imagining everyone would respect and fear him.*

**Dorothy:** Your Majesty, if you were king, you wouldn't be afraid of anything?

**Cowardly Lion:** Not nobody! Not no how!

**Tin Woodsman:** Not even a rhinoceros?

**Cowardly Lion:** Imposerous!

**Dorothy:** How about a hippopotamus?

**Cowardly Lion:** Why, I'd thrash him from top to "bottomus"!

**Dorothy:** Supposing you met an elephant?

**Cowardly Lion:** I'd wrap him up in cellophane!

 **Scarecrow:** What if it were a brontosaurus?

**Cowardly Lion:** I'd show him who was king of the forest!

**LOVE IT!**

# 12

# THE CRITICISM YOU DECIDE TO USE

*He who ignores criticism will end in poverty and disgrace; if you accept criticism, you will be honored.* (Proverbs 13:18 paraphrased)

In this life, be prepared for people to criticize, especially, if you plan on doing anything important. When you take a stand and begin to succeed, you will be positioned above the norm, or above mediocrity; in this place, listening to critics must cease. Because you are no longer invisible, people believe they have permission to scrutinize what you do. This should not happen, but increased success brings increased accusations. Decide right now to silence the voice of criticism.

***Those who endure criticism are those who will succeed beyond the negativity.***

***"If you're not big enough to stand criticism then you are too small to be praised." Abraham Lincoln***

*Criticism is the death gargle of a non-achiever.*

Those who feel the need to complain are usually those who haven't made an attempt to do anything themselves.

It is wise to endure those who talk about you as well as those who make snide remarks about you. You are climbing your way to the top, so expect critics to be angry.

Decide, right now, you're not going to leave the chariot with the king in order to answer the critic in the crowd. Never leave the presence of success so you can chase the one who throws tomatoes in the crowd. Your future is attached to your willingness to endure the critics. How do you silence a critic? By enduring their criticism, then, succeeding.

## HOW TO HANDLE CRITICISM:

- If it's untrue… Disregard it.
- If it's unfair…. Don't let it irritate you.
- If it's ignorant… Smile and move on.
- If it's justified… learn from it.

The Bible says, "Judge not lest you be judged." (Matthew 7:1) Criticism is the act of passing judgment as to the merits of anything; it is finding fault with something, or someone. The **"art of rejection,"** is when someone rejects what you say, or what you look like. An example is not being picked from the lineup because of your appearance. However, the **"rejection of art,"** is rejecting what you are gifted to do. This type of rejection cuts deep due to the focus, of the criticism, being aimed directly at one's inner self. It is the gifting being critiqued, then, shunned. The proof of your next season begins when the critics change their focus from your external appearance to your internal gifting. Those who succeed don't allow others to change how they see themselves. So, be cautious, enjoy success, but also retain the opinion you have of yourself.

# 31 Favored Decisions

# 13

## THE CHARACTER YOU DECIDE TO DEVELOP

---

**"Development is what you do in private, it is what you do in the dark. Character is what you do in the light."**

*"What lies behind us and what lies before us are small matters compared to what lies within us." Ralph Waldo Emerson*

***Character is what is inside a person and is revealed by that person's action.***

Good character includes virtues such as honesty, courage, and integrity. I can usually tell what's going on inside a person by looking at how they respond to what's going on around them. Most often, it is a good indicator of what's, actually, going on inside their thinking. An example would be someone with a cluttered mind, they usually live in a cluttered world.

When I think of Joseph, in the book of Genesis, I see these keys to his success.

## The Coat of Favor

Though Joseph's father had given him the coat of favor, or the coat of many colors, he had not yet developed the character of favor.

## Conduct of Favor

After Joseph's, jealous, brothers threw him into a pit, he was sold to Ishmaelite traders who were heading to Egypt. Joseph never complained, even after, being sold to Potiphar, an officer of Pharaoh. Because God was with Joseph, he succeeded in everything he did. He was put in charge of his master's household, and property, and God blessed Potiphar as a result. Because Potiphar saw how everything prospered in Joseph's hand, he gave him complete control over everything he owned. When Potiphar's wife accused him of a wicked thing, he was arrested and thrown in prison. God blessed him, yet again, and He caused everything Joseph did to prosper. As a result, Joseph was put in charge of all the prisoners as well as over everything that took place in the prison. During Joseph's prison sentence, the Pharaoh's cup-bearer and baker were thrown in prison as well. While locked up, both had dreams causing their countenance to fall. So, Joseph reaches out to help.

## The Character of Favor

The ability to help someone while dealing with your own trouble reveals your readiness for God's next step.

*Character is developed in the middle of failure, crisis and loss...*

God will use every storm, not to destroy, but to build

character.

*"Character cannot be developed in ease and quiet. Only through experience of trial and suffering can the soul be strengthened, vision cleared, ambition inspired, and success achieved."* — *Helen Keller,*

Character is the power, of the inner man, to direct the soul in obedience to a decision. Your soul is made up of the mind, will, and emotions. Character reveals content, or the power of solid, stable living. To develop strong character makes for a better future and can bring greater success.

# 31 Favored Decisions

# 14

# THE UNHAPPINESS YOU DECIDE TO OVERCOME

Depression is a sickness of the mind; a gloomy sadness that lurks within. I don't offer a treatment for the depressed, however, I make an attempt to encourage people so they can deal with it. For those whose depression is medical in nature, there are medical doctors that can help recalibrate the chemical imbalance. For the rest of us, this chapter is for us!

Due to the high stress levels, in our world, along with the crazy time schedules, depression seems to be at an all-time high. Before those low, sad feelings take over, Stop! Take a time out, lift up your hands, and immediately sing praise to the Lord.

- Shifting your mood is a great weapon against depression.
- Taking charge of your feelings can redirect your focus.

- Eliminating wrong thoughts can stop the feelings

of depression.

In most cases, depression is an unrealistic thought pattern that begins to create hopeless feelings regarding the present circumstance.

### *Most people live at the mercy of their circumstances...*

It is always necessary to fight feelings of depression. This is done by rejecting unrealistic thought patterns, then, retraining yourself with good, uplifting thoughts. Philippians 4:8 states, "...whatsoever things are lovely...think on these things." So, when depression manifests, read and meditate on this scripture. Then, I believe, depression will leave.

People have the tendency to attach sadness to things instead of fighting to correct what is going on in the mind. This can be dangerous. With depression, blaming is, usually, the first thing people do. And, when life isn't going according to our desires, it is easy to attack those closest to us. Depressed people believe that changing the people around them will make them happier. However, this is not the case, because, after all the attacks, they are still depressed and unhappy. Due to its illusive nature, chasing happiness can be very frustrating, and exhausting. Happiness is a feeling, not a destination, therefore, it can't be caught.

What is needed is an internal awakening, not another emotional fix. It is possible to have joy in the midst of an unhappy situation; and, joy is key for coming out of depression. Real joy is **supernatural** and can be unlocked by the presence of the Spirit of God. There is no substitute for supernatural JOY!

*Worry is confidence in your adversary and can create depression.*

# 31 Favored Decisions

# 15

# THE DISAPPOINTMENTS YOU DECIDE TO GET OVER

Disappointment is sadness, or displeasure, caused by the nonfulfillment of one's hopes, or expectations. It can be a daily occurrence and, unfortunately, no one is exempt from its grasp. When disappointment comes, it can intensify by other events transpiring throughout the course of the day. "When it rains, it pours." Disappointment is a devious emotion that can become life-altering. It is closely followed by stress and must be dealt with.

Disappointment comes by putting wrong expectations on others, or events. The One thing, or Person, that will never disappoint is the Holy Spirit. Put your expectations in Him! Because nothing is impossible with God, you can also place your hope in Him. You can Trust that He is able to heal; He is able to satisfy; and, He is able to deliver.

## Maneuvering through disappointment

- *Take a moment to feel the emotion*
  Tina Gilbertson, LPC, DCC, Psychotherapist stated, *"When you get bad news, take a moment to let it sink in."* Let the emotion express itself, it's okay to

experience the disappointment. Ms. Gilbertson also states, *"Find a word for how you feel, such as disappointed, resentful, or afraid. Labeling feelings will allow you to make a cool-headed decision about what to do next."* It is not a sin to be disappointed, nor is it wrong to release the emotions that come as a result of the disappointment.

- *Do a reality check*
  It is not as bad as it appears; wallow and get back up with new perspective. Though it feels like the most horrible thing that could happen, it is only a feeling. And because people can be more dramatic than necessary, those feelings are most likely not true. Take a step back, objectively analyze the situation, and separate fact from fiction. Then, reduce or eliminate the negative self-talk.

- *Take the high road when hit below the waist*
  Without any notice, crisis can happen. Our reactions, though, will determine how we move through those situations. However, to respond is better than to react. Make the decision to speak positive words and avoid all negativity in the midst of the crisis. Let your mind be free of all negative thinking.

- *Don't obsessively dwell on negativity*
  Turning away from disappointment is the power necessary to achieve a good outcome. However, the longer discouragement has a place to occupy, depression can set in. Don't allow the situation to overwhelm you, but make the decision to learn, as well as to grow, through that experience. By changing how you think about the crisis, it will help to restore a sense of peace to your mind.

- *Avoid taking out your frustrations on others*
Feeling disappointed can cause you to be cynical and critical of others. This is not a good reaction and it is to be avoided. Because cynicism and criticism can cause disconnection from others, it is necessary to build a learning platform for growth instead.

- *Put things in proper perspective*
Each person interprets their circumstances through the lens of what has actually happened. The goal is to learn how to win when it looks like a loss. At the same time, you should trust that God can turn a setback into a comeback. In order to reframe your world, it is good to find positive, life-learning lessons in every disappointment. Being productive as well as positive goes a long way in helping to win the battle over disappointment.

- *Refrain from taking people's opinions, and reactions, to heart*
Wise people understand that people have unique perspectives when observing certain situations. However, not all are wise. It is important to monitor the voices allowed in your world; those opinions may not always be right.

- *Avoid those who magnify disappointment*
Because we all want to be heard, it brings an element of relief when we can share our disappointments with others. It is important, though, to avoid sharing with those who constantly blame and want to put a negative spin on everything. People who vomit negativity should be avoided, or at the least, there should be limited contact. When dealing with your own disappointments, let negative talk go in one ear and out the other.

- ***Develop your mind with positive thinking***
  Your mind is a muscle, train it! Our minds are fundamentally wired to focus on the negatives; however, the mind is trainable and can be rewired. Write a gratitude list and read it daily. Train your brain to reign in the realm of the positive rather than wallow in the darkness of negativity. By learning to control how you think, you will be more equipped to control what is in your world.

- ***Calm your mind and see clearly***
  During stressful situations, the emotional center of the brain is able to override our ability to process. It is important, during those times, to calm your mind in order to make clear decisions. During stressful moments, anxiety increases along with your heart rate. The mind also shuts down and it reverts to survival mode. In this situation, remember to settle your mind, then, regain control.

In the midst of crisis, the Holy Spirit has impressed me to:

**Stay cool, stay calm, and stay Kingdom!**

## Seven Keys to Manage a Crisis

- Maintain an attitude of worship.
- Have continuous conversations with the Holy Spirit.
- Settle your mind and prevent panicking.
- Rebuke the voice of fear and receive faith's voice.
- Change fearful thoughts into warrior thoughts.
- Don't allow thoughts of failure to take root. God is your strength.

- Prepare your spirit and receive the divine will of God.

Remember, you are never alone; God is with you and has promised to never leave you. He has sent Holy Spirit into the world to comfort, counsel, and guide those who trust Him.

# 31 Favored Decisions

# 16

## THE STORM YOU DECIDE TO SURVIVE

◆――――――――――――◆

Every human has experienced storms and they usually don't happen at a good time. There are moments of freedom, but then the storm clouds appear and damage is a probability. Because storms aren't scheduled, they are likely to interfere with your predetermined plans.

Can you think of a time when a storm stopped your weekend adventure? Maybe you planned a picnic, a boat ride, or spending the day at the lake, or beach. It was blue sky on the way to your intended destination but, upon arrival, the storm clouds began to darken. The weather forecast did not include a chance of rain, however, without warning; wind, rain, and destruction were unleashed. Learning how to deal with the storms of life is necessary for achieving success.

### Storms Redirect You to a Better Future

Unexpected storms will not destroy you, however, they can redirect you to a better future. In Mark 6:45-53, Jesus had His disciples get into a boat traveling to Bethsaida; He sent them ahead. In Greek, Bethsaida means to hunt, to pursue, to seek, or to chase. After leaving Jesus, the disciples began having difficulty rowing the boat due to the wind being against them. When Jesus saw them struggling, He walked towards them on the water. However, they became even more scared because Jesus appeared to be a ghost. This prompted Jesus' command to be courageous; then, He Himself got in the boat with His disciples. Afterwards, they ended up in Gennesaret which is a place of rest and peace, or paradise; Gennesaret means harp or lyre. The disciples were no longer chasing, or pursuing, but had been redirected by the storm to a better place. By staying afloat, and outlasting the wind, the waves, and the rain, we can have the same results. Allow me to break this down

.

***Submit to the vehicle as well as the direction of a divine instruction.***

Following instructions is vital to reaching the desired destination. Because many people refuse to obey the Lord, a good, end result is usually not obtained. The journey may not be a pleasant one, however, it will end up well when the instructions are followed.

***The storm doesn't always show up until half way through the journey.***

Storms can be an indicator you are on the right path. They can also be a huge distraction meant to discourage and destroy the purpose of the journey. No matter what, decide to survive the storm as well as the debris it causes. In the middle of the storm, it takes the same effort to go forward, as back. Which will you choose? My hope is that you would continue forward.

### *Jesus doesn't show up until the fourth watch.*

The fourth watch is the last watch of the night. It is a time to hang on, and endure, because this is when Jesus shows up. Psalms 30:5 states, "Weeping may endure for a night, but joy comes in the morning." Miracles generally happen at the end of a crisis, not at the beginning. So, it is necessary to outlast, out maneuver, and overcome the first three watches of the night. Do what it takes to make it to the other side of the fourth watch!

### *The fourth watch!*

Jesus walked on water and was not affected by the storm. He also didn't see the disciples as part of the storm, or the struggle. However, Mark 6:49 states, "but when they saw Him walking on the lake, they thought it was a ghost and let out a shriek." Jesus heard them, and they made it to the other side. Don't forget, praise is a vital part of any victory; in the midst of praise, storms lose their strength. Remember, what we speak during the battle will determine whether we face victory, or end in defeat.

# 31 Favored Decisions

# 17

# THE TRAINING
# YOU DECIDE
# TO ENDURE

*"The best training program in the world is absolutely worthless without the will to execute it properly, consistently, and with intensity."* John Romaniello

Man's future is determined by the training he receives; people will never improve without it. A person's monetary value is not determined by their material possessions but by their level of training. Unfortunately, the majority of people can be too lazy, or stubborn, to obtain the education needed for greater advancements.

While in Jacksonville, Florida, Dr. Mike Murdock began questioning me on the topic of guard dogs; he was interested in buying one. I was bewildered by the questions, however, I did the research and discovered where to find the type of dog he was interested in. Dr. Murdock flew to a school in Orlando, Florida, and talked to the instructors about several dogs. The first dog was trained but, due to memory issues, would always need to be retrained. The second dog had incredible memory skills and would never need retraining, however, it was not kid-friendly. Not only that, this dog could not distinguish between child and assailant; it would need to stay on a leash. These two dogs were ugly and very unfriendly. The third dog was uglier than the first two, however, he was highly trained; and, he would never need to be retrained. This dog was able to tell the difference between a harmless child and an aggressor. He was also able to move in and out of guard dog mode easily. The cost of these dogs ranged from $2500 - $10,000. After their discussion on the three dogs, Dr. Murdock asked about the happy, playful puppy he saw as he arrived at the school. The owners stated that the puppy was not trainable, would be free of cost, and could be taken home that day. Dr. Murdock learned that their value was determined by their training, not how cute or pleasant they were. The difference between the free puppy and the $10,000 dog was TRAINING! Training is the ability and the willingness to learn. And, learners have the desire to be trained.

*"The capacity to learn is a gift, the ability to learn is a skill and, the willingness to learn is a choice." Brian Herbert*

*Your Future is decided by the learning curve you can endure.*

*Endurance is a Qualifier.*

# 18

# THE FUTURE
# YOU DECIDE TO
# WALK IN

No one can enter their future carrying their past. Everyone has a past and what they do with it can determine what takes place tomorrow.

Everyone has two choices: 1) make no changes and continue doing the same thing; or 2) determine what changes are needed and make them today. With the one, the future will look like the present. But, with the second, it is possible to create a different tomorrow. Change is never easy but, for a better future, it is worth the effort.

The present is made up of moments and events. As a matter of fact, a person's life also consists of moments and events. I was once asked, "What was your defining moment?" I answered, "I can't see just one moment defining where I am today." If one moment is able to cause success in the present, then one moment can cancel that success in the future. Our lives are more than a moment, they are many moments with many events. They can be good ones, God ones, or bad ones; it is within your ability to choose how you are defined in those events. It is our responsibility to control the meaning of the moment, thereby, preventing it from controlling us. Bad moments can become great moments by refusing to allow opportunity for bitterness.

The future doesn't happen without our involvement; tomorrow is still scheduled and the decisions that are made today can positively, or negatively, effect the future. So, be diligent and get involved with all your tomorrows by making wise decisions today.

*Struggle always surrounds a great future!*

# 19

# THE STRUGGLE YOU DECIDE TO EMBRACE

◆───────────────────────────────◆

*"Struggle produces strength."*

"Nothing great comes to our lives without struggle," and, "The proof you are changing is in the struggle."

Struggle is not fun and can take lots of mind power, and energy, to see it through to the end. It is hard to understand but there is purpose in every struggle.

After completing two Christian Network Television interviews, I flew from Detroit, Michigan, to New York City. I was scheduled to speak on the Trinity Broadcasting Network as well as preach at a church in Mt. Vernon, New York. As I rested on the plane, I asked the Holy Spirit, **"Why is everything in my life such a struggle? Why does it seem that everything takes longer for me?"** As I felt the weight of those questions flowing from my eyes, the Holy Spirit spoke saying, "STRUGGLE IS

NECESSARY." That was not what I wanted to hear.

## *"Struggle produces Strength. "*

Success without struggle is never going to happen. This is a hard truth to understand but success requires struggle. Growing pains are a benefit to the budding business, not a hindrance. Struggle stretches and matures us but we have to allow the growth.

While I was still on the plane, headed to New York, I received this word from the Lord. He said,

*"Son, when I size up your destiny, and your future, I evaluate how much strength you're going to require in order to maintain, and conquer, your future. Then, I begin to let struggle and opposition build the necessary spiritual and mental muscle you're going to need to have it!"*

I don't know what you are going through, or what you have survived, but you can get through it. You not only have the opportunity to get through every struggle, you can also thrive in the middle of those ordeals.

Be very careful that you don't misinterpret the struggle; unnecessary energy and effort are applied as a result. Not every struggle is:

- A storm
- An attack
- A crisis
- A problem

- A failure

Struggle can occur as a result of people becoming more qualified than that of their present season. In other words, growth has occurred. Expansion, advancement, and moving forward can now take place. However, by allowing the enemy to cause a misinterpretation of the struggle, valuable time and focus will be wasted on fighting, and resisting, a false reality. Don't hesitate to Move when the need for greater maturity is discovered. When one level is satisfied, go for the next. Don't stay for comfort, allow the struggle. Your future is always better than the effort exerted to get there. Your future starts now!

# 31 Favored Decisions

# 20

# THE VOW YOU DECIDED TO HONOR

$\blacklozenge$————————————————$\blacklozenge$

This may sound crazy, but I believe a vow is stronger than a seed. A vow is a solemn promise to God committing oneself to an act, service, or condition. It is a promise to do something after God gives what has been asked of Him. For instance, after hearing of the financial needs of a building project, my desire was to give a $5,000 seed. However, at that moment, I did not have $5,000. So, I made a vow to God saying, "I will give the money for this building project, if it is provided." God hears this type of vow and is able to partner with you to get the project completed.

## Two Kinds of Vows

There are two types of vows. The first follows the above example where a partnership is formed between the person and God. With this vow, God and man work together to bring about the completion of a project. Without this joining together, it might have been impossible to accomplish. There are many successful stories of people who made such vows. One example involves the owner of JC Penny who vowed to live off a tenth of his income, a tithe, while giving God the other ninety percent for the success of his business. At the age of sixty-five, Colonel Sanders vowed that, if God would bless his chicken recipe, he would give God ten percent of all the profits. In their day, this partnership was very successful because they kept their vow to God.

The second involves making a vow for the success of your activities. In the Bible, there is a story of a man named Jacob. After fleeing from his brother Esau, Jacob fell asleep in the desert, completely broken. While sleeping, he dreamed of a window opening into the heavenlies with angels ascending and descending a ladder which had reached down to the earth. Jacob made God a vow:

*20) And Jacob vowed a vow, saying, If God will be with me, and will keep me in this way that I go, and will give me bread to eat, and raiment to put on, 22) and this stone, which I have set for a pillar, shall be God's house: and of all that thou shalt give me **I will surely give the tenth unto thee**.* (Genesis 28:20 & 22 KJV)

In my opinion, Jacob placed a demand on God to oversee the success of his activities. Making vows are very serious to God. However, too many people make vows in the heat of the moment; when life gets easier, the vow is forgotten. Because God is offended when vows are not kept, this makes for a very bad decision.

*"When you make a vow to the LORD your God, you shall not delay to pay it, for it would be sin in you, and the LORD*

*your God will surely require it of you. "However, if you refrain from vowing, it would not be sin in you. "You shall be careful to perform what goes out from your lips, just as you have voluntarily vowed to the LORD your God, what you have promised.* (Deuteronomy 23:21-23)

# 31 Favored Decisions

# 21

# THE GRATITUDE YOU DECIDE TO SHOW

Thankfulness is the password for entry. And, to be thankful, or grateful, can be the hardest thing to maintain throughout the day. For me, I can become overwhelmed in the course of my day; and, instead of being grateful, I become depressed. In general, people battle with mental negativity while most struggle with being thankful. However, the biggest key for overcoming this issue is "the rebound." Rebounding is easier when focus turns from the thing causing depression, and, instead, turning towards the Lord with praise and thanksgiving.

Gratitude is definitely a decision, not a feeling. Being thankful is different than feeling thankful; and, feeling thankful isn't always going to happen. In order to maintain a good, thankful attitude, one must make the decision to stay in that frame of mind.

There are times we find ourselves in a sea of struggle and disappointment. After evaluating the present season, we notice that age has crept up on us and we realize that our goals have not been met. All of a sudden, an overwhelming sadness covers us, like a blanket, allowing depression and discouragement to have a voice. As a result, the mind begins to drift to the things that could have been, or should have been, but are not. This is where being thankful is challenged. Make the decision to keep a positive frame of mind in order to avoid coming into agreement with negativity. Stop focusing on wrong emotions and begin to focus on the blessings you do have. Be assured, there is much to be thankful for!

As of this writing, my friend, Robert Michael, has been fighting cancer for fourteen months. His doctors have recently informed him that he should already be dead. Cancer was growing in his neck and was threatening to choke the life out of him. Thankfully, after receiving help from medical professionals, the cancer began shrinking. Unfortunately, after the completion of all treatments, it resumed its growth again. This pattern happened several times bringing encouragement, then disappointment. While watching Robert battle this vile thing called cancer, I did not hear him make one complaint. He has not questioned, "why me?" Though he has un-imaginable pain that shoots through the back of his head, he has not stopped working. Through all of the pain, he continues to help clean, paint, remodel, or anything he'. In the midst of this troubling sickness, Robert continues to serve God; for this, he is to be commended.

Robert's courage, strength and, willingness is a testimony to what can be accomplished by maintaining a grateful attitude. With tears, he continues to lift his hands in order to praise and worship His Father in Heaven. To this day, I am honored to call him friend.

Gratitude is a decision, a weapon, that hell has no wisdom to combat. No matter what goes on in this world, it is important to stay in a thankful attitude. As a result, we are open for the empowerment that brings incredible peace and joy. Being grateful charges the atmosphere with favor, it is always a blessing.

# 31 Favored Decisions

# 22

# THE COUNTENANCE YOU DECIDE TO PROTECT

---

**Countenance is a decision, not a feeling!**

Countenance is defined as a facial expression, a look, an appearance.

*People see you before they hear you.*

Your posture, facial expressions, and appearance reveal more than you think. I used to say it this way, "Dress for Success." Today, appearance can include wearing skinny jeans, t-shirts, and baggy clothes; it should also include a good countenance. Countenance is a discipline that should be practiced and maintained in order to look successful.

**Countenance is power...**

In Genesis 4, God approached Cain with an interesting question, *"And the Lord said unto Cain, why art thou wroth? And why is thy countenance fallen?"* Countenance is important and should be controlled. So, when God noticed Cain's fallen countenance, He knew something was wrong. Cain's facial expressions and his body language were revealing the negativity flowing through his mind. It is important to understand that God was not the only one watching Cain's face, Satan was as well.

## Countenance Reveals YOU!

If you have a terrible countenance, everyone can see it, including Satan. He pays attention to countenance as well as body language. As I was growing up, my Dad would always focus on my posture. He would say to me, "sit up," "pick up your feet," or "stop slouching." He was training me to appear confident through my body language. What is your posture revealing? As Kingdom people, we are to walk in power, and authority, filled with the Spirit of God. The Bible states that the strength of the Lord is joy; which is available for every situation. However, the majority of professed believers seem to be defeated and depressed rather than full of joy and victory. Defeat and depression show in a person's countenance. Why? What happened to the strength of the Lord? As an act of faith, it is important to allow His joy to reflect through your countenance and to work through your body language. For,

- Countenance opens doors.
- Countenance gives access to millionaires.
- Countenance creates energy in others.
- Countenance is a weapon for negotiation.

In Genesis, when God saw Cain's countenance, He warned

him that the enemy was monitoring, or studying, his facial expressions. God made a bold declaration by stating that Cain could rule over the enemy of his soul; he could resist the enemy's temptations and overcome. By guarding his countenance, his attitude, Cain could gain victory over his opponent. Failure is inevitable without a good countenance.

# 31 Favored Decisions

# 23

# THE GREED YOU DECIDE TO MASTER

◆———————————————————◆

The dictionary defines greed as an overwhelming urge to have more of something, usually more than really needed. Greed is often connected with money; it is a desire to acquire as much of it as possible. In Psychology Today, Michael W. Austin Ph.D. states, "It is foremost a matter of the heart, of our inner lives. Greed is an excessive love or desire for money or possessions, but caring too much about them. A greedy person is too attached to his things and his money, or he desires more money and more things in an excessive way. Greed has unpleasant effects on our inner emotional lives." The drive behind greed can urge people to lust after anything, including food, material possessions, better jobs, etc.

To have overwhelming urges for more, or to have more than usually needed, can be a Godly characteristic as well. This is especially true, if the desire for more includes being a blessing to others, or the Kingdom of God; being equipped to help people is never a bad thing. However, when selfishness interferes with being a blessing, the evil side of greed becomes apparent. This type of greed motivates the mistreatment of others; it makes them feel less than because you have more. If an individual's identity is driven by competition for more, it could be influenced by a spirit of greed.

During a trip to Ghana, Africa, I visited the Slave Forts where the Transatlantic Slave industry began; I was with my friend, Bishop Domonic Allotey, In the slave trading days, many African men, women and children were captured, then brought here and sold into slavery. They were shipped, in horrendous conditions, across the Atlantic to other countries. Unfortunately, many of them died before reaching their destination. Not only were the conditions horrific on the ships, but their treatment was less than human. It was heartrending to listen to the, actual, stories of what man could do to another man. Men, who were not meant to be slaves, had to endure being stolen from their families, rejection by other men, abuse of every kind, humiliation, unimaginable punishment, and degradation; this kind of treatment is meant, only, for the devil. During the tour, a lady from the United States yelled out, *"Makes me want to kill white people."* As the only white person in the crowd, imagine how that statement affected me as well as the others on this tour. The Guide recognized, by her words, she was a black American who believed that white people were to blame for slavery and racism. This is a common belief in America. In reality, racism had nothing to do with slavery. The tour guide stated, "America was one of the last nations to enter the slave trade industry and one of the last to stop this practice." The woman became angry, and confused, prompting her to ask, "Then, if it wasn't racism, what caused slavery?" While looking at the people, the tour guide stated, **"IT WAS GREED."**

It was greed that prompted one man to put another man in bondage. One African tribe captured, and sold, their rival African tribe who was then sent across the Atlantic never to be seen again. Afterwards, the remaining tribe would take over, or possess, the territory that was left behind. They were able to capitalize on the misfortune of their rivals, thereby, increasing in wealth; a true picture of greed. So, in order to resolve the issue of racism, greed must be addressed. The jealousy and anger birthed from the acts of greed must also be addressed. Cain exampled the type of greed which produced an anger enabling him to rise up and kill his brother, Abel.

The synonyms for greed include:

- Materialism
- Devouring
- Gluttonous
- Ravenous
- Voracious
- Self-Centered

The term ravenous means, intensely eager for gratification or satisfaction. In the bible, we are told there are ravenous wolves living among us. Here, I believe God is warning us about greedy, self-centered, people who will devour for materialistic gain. This is GREED!

## *How do you conquer, and master, greed?*

- Be a giver! The cure for greed is giving. The bible makes it clear, "*it is more blessed to give than to receive.*" (Acts 20:35) *"Therefore, do not be hesitant to give to others because God loves a cheerful giver."* (2 Corinthians 9:7) However, make sure your intention of giving is to bless others—not to gain more for yourself.

- Remember, be grateful to those who have been generous to you.

- Don't be an island; live with others in mind. Desire to increase so others can benefit from your excess.

- Understand that you could be the answer to someone's prayers. Don't just pray for someone's financial need, give them money as well.

# 24

# THE INSTRUCTION YOU DECIDE TO FOLLOW

---

*The instructions you choose to follow will decide your next season.*

*Instructions are the building blocks for the success of any organization.*

Those who follow instructions will be more prosperous than those who don't; especially if they so with passion and excellence.

Every documented miracle, in the Bible, was preceded by an instruction: *"Wash yourself in the pool," "Go dip seven times in the Jordan,"* and, *"Borrow pots, not a few but many."* By God's instruction, Elijah went to the widow's house on the back of a great famine. He informed Elijah that, at the widow's house, He would feed and care for him. Upon arriving at her house, Elijah discovered she wasn't rich or flowing in abundance. Regardless, Elijah asked, *"Please bring a little water in a container for me to drink."* He also asked, *"Please bring me a piece of bread in your hand."* The widow replied, *"As Adonai your God lives, I have nothing baked, only a handful of meal in a pot and a little oil in the jug. Here I am, gathering a couple sticks of wood, so that I can go and cook it for myself and my son. After we have eaten that, we will die."* Then, Elijah gives her an instruction, *"Don't be afraid. Go; and do what you said; but first, use a little of it to make me a small loaf of bread; and bring it out to me. After that, make food for yourself and your son."* Elijah proceeded to say, *"For this is what Adonai the God of Israel says: 'The pot of meal will not get used up, nor will there fail to be oil in the jug, until the day Adonai sends rain down on the land.'"* The widow believed the word of the prophet, obediently followed his instruction, and reaped the harvest spoken by Elijah. As a result, the famine did not destroy her, her son, or her house. For, *"The pot of meal did not get used up, nor did there fail to be oil in the jug."* (1 Kings 17:1-16)

- Obeyed *instructions* unlock the golden door of supply.
- Obeyed *instructions* decide the unity, and fluidity, of a miracle.
- The difference between what you are experiencing and what you could be experiencing, is an *instruction*.
- The *instructions* followed will unlock the future you are destined to walk.

I have learned to listen and follow an instruction to its completion; this maintains an open door for connection to my mentor.

In John 8:28-32, Jesus states,

*"When you raise up the Son of Man, then you will know who I am—that I'm not making this up but speaking only what the Father taught me. The One who sent me stays with me. He doesn't abandon me. He sees how much joy I take in pleasing him."[30] When he put it in these terms, many people decided to believe. [31-32] Then Jesus turned to the Jews who had claimed to believe in him. "If you stick with this, living out what I tell you, you are my disciples for sure. Then you will experience for yourselves the truth, and the truth will free you."* (MSG Bible; Bible Gateway website)

Jesus was indicating He wasn't doing anything on His own, or for selfish gain; however, He was following the teachings, and instructions, of the **Father**. The Father was His source.  He then made this famous quote, *"If you follow these instructions, you will experience the truth. You will live them out. You will obey them, and they will in turn make you free!"*

Again, every miracle is preceded by an instruction. The one who carries out instructions lives a life that has been made free. When God speaks to people, it is generally with an instruction; Genesis 2:16, *"And the Lord God commanded the man."* From the beginning God gave Adam instructions. Unfortunately, the Fall of Man happened because Adam disobeyed the instruction, *"do not eat from the tree of the knowledge of good and evil."* Rules are in place to protect man, not to punish him. And, disobeyed rules can be very costly, as it was to Adam's family, and to ours. It is always important to maintain right words, and make right decisions, without allowing feelings to get in the way. Following God's counsel, through His Word, even when difficult, will prove to be life's greatest blessing.

# 25

# THE INJUSTICE YOU DECIDE TO MOVE PAST

*Injustice anywhere is a threat to justice everywhere."*
Martin Luther King Jr.

*"Each time a man stands up for an ideal, or acts to improve the lot of others, or strikes out against injustice, he sends forth a tiny ripple of hope, and crossing each other from a million different centers of energy and daring those ripples build a current which can sweep down the mightiest walls of oppression and resistance."* Robert F. Kennedy

There is no escaping injustice; it is the violation of the rights of others. It is the unjust, or unfair treatment, that is hard to hide from; it is almost impossible to be free of its effects. In this day of divisiveness and disagreement, injustice is a sensitive subject. And, in the face of injustice, it is important how you react. Will you allow those who inflicted unfair treatment to control the situation? Will you rise above the violation of your rights? Or, will you be buried beneath the injustice committed?

The problem with the word, injustice, is that you don't really know its application, nor is it always understood. A right decision is hard to make without understanding what really caused the injustice.

## There are different kinds of injustice

- **People Injustice** is when an individual, or a group of people, treat another individual, or group, wrongly.

- **Environmental Injustice** is when bad things happen to good people. Remember, injustice means, "unfairness." Mother Nature can unleash her atmospheric fury, at any time, and cannot be stopped, or controlled, by man. The news is full of this type of injustice which can include forest fires, hurricanes and typhoons, snowstorms, tornadoes, rain, winds, and mudslides to name a few. These events are not selective, nor do they show mercy, but they can be very deadly.

- **Physical injustice** happens when your body becomes sick. This type of injustice comes unexpectedly for no reason at all. There are people who are, extremely, conscious of healthy eating and exercising, however, though they did everything necessary to live longer, they died without warning.

As unfair as injustice is, every human being is subject to its harm; it cannot be controlled by man. However, when the storms of life hit, determine to walk in a place of victory; walk, believing you have the power of success, joy, and peace to help you through. Injustice may rear its ugly head, however, succumbing to hopelessness is not an option.

Injustices can develop into strongholds of the mind, imprisoning the individual to a life controlled by its oppressive nature.

## Overcoming Injustice Mindsets

- **Victim mindsets** can imprison the individual for life. This mindset has a blame mentality which causes the person to become stuck. Fight this mentality and turn it into a victory.

- **Excuse mindsets** are the nails that build a house of failure. Stop making excuses and move into your future. People who always make excuses are not happy people.

- **Informative mindsets** are information seekers who easily become addicted to knowledge. They find it difficult to find success because they are always learning but never achieving. Achievers are those who have learned to act on the information they have uncovered.

- **Executioner mindsets** are those that explode into new places and ideas; they execute the plan as it is learned.

# 26

# THE GREATNESS YOU DECIDE TO RECOGNIZE

The Word of God teaches us to honor our parents, to honor those who teach us, and to honor those who have authority over us. However, we were never taught how to recognize or honor greatness. It seems natural to exalt those who earn that distinction, unfortunately, in many cases, we neglect to do so.

When I speak about greatness, I am not just referring to a person's accomplishments, or the heights they have achieved. I am speaking of the seed of greatness, hidden, in the heart of everyone reading this book.

Robert Cooper's book, "Executive EQ: Emotional Intelligence in Business," contains a beautiful story about a little boy from Tibet. During Cooper's visit, the child taught him the traditional greeting, "Tashi Deleh." When translated means, "I honor the greatness within you." The child asked, "How do people greet one another in

America? Does 'Hello' have the same meaning as it does in Tibet?"

Imagine how different our world would be if we would recognize, and honor, the greatness in others. And, how great it would be if we would acknowledge the importance of others. Taking a moment to admire the beauty within ourselves, and one another, is a powerful practice. I Corinthians 13:7 tells us, love looks for the best in others. Love empowers us to see the greatness in all human beings. Love can change the direction of a conversation, a meeting, or a relationship. How we seek to love, or honor, others will determine how God will honor us.

It is hard to accept that we are living in a world that appears to be moving backwards rather than forward. Why has this happened? Why are we watching people destroy each other? Could it be we've forgotten how to recognize the Divine Greatness God has placed within man. When we walk according to the rules and principles of the Kingdom of God, we stop seeing the outer shell of the person and, instead, we begin seeing all the good God intended for mankind. It is important to note, what a person continuously looks at will eventually become their truth, even if it is completely false. If all that is seen, or heard, is based on the news, the riots, the voices of negativity, etc., then, people are feeding off of an agenda meant for the destruction of the soul. What is fed into the soul, through the senses, creates a reality that blocks what God intended man to see, *"The treasures of heaven hidden in earthen vessels."* (2 Corinthians 4:7)

By looking past, or avoiding, those soul-destroying things,

we would discover the seed of greatness is always hidden in something the carnal man would criticize. For the natural mind cannot discern the things born of the Spirit of God.

## Where has God Hidden His Treasures?

- God hid His treasures within man's heart. *"But we have this treasure in earthen vessels, that the excellency of the Power may be of God."* (2 Corinthians 4:7)

- God hid His treasures in darkness. *"I will give you the hidden treasures, riches stored in secret places, so that you may know that I am the LORD, the God of Israel, who summons you by name."* (Isaiah 45:3, NIV). God places great things in what we would call wrong places. He hides His riches in the secret places of man.

- God has hidden His powerful, great treasures in plain sight. It is sad to say, much of mankind will spend the majority of their lives looking for what God has already placed within them. God's riches, His seed of greatness, is hidden in all of us. The person who comes to recognize that seed, then honor it, will unlock its value.

It is important to understand, most treasure is hidden in dark, damp, and sometimes hard places. The ones who are willing to do what it takes to discover what He considers to be Gold and Greatness, will also enjoy the rewards of the search. They will see, and understand, the value placed within every human spirit.

Be determined to look for, and appreciate, the greatness in every person. Make it a life goal to dig out, and honor, what God has hidden; unlocking a season of His excellent favor. God's Kingdom doesn't see color or race, it looks past cultural differences as well as politics. His Kingdom is revealed when a group of people come together for the purpose of unlocking, recognizing, and honoring each of mankind's unique characteristics implanted for the good of all people. This makes up His treasures.

# 27

# THE FAVOR YOU DECIDE TO RECOGNIZE

---

*"Anything unrecognized will go uncelebrated, anything uncelebrated will go unrewarded, and anything that is unrewarded will exit your life."*
Dr. Mike Murdock

**Favor is not luck.**
Favor is not a lucky moment; it is given, by God, to help people live successful lives. *All success is attached to favor.*

**Favor is a seed before the Harvest!**
The difference between favor, and famine, is the ability to recognize favor. What is favor's purpose? Where is favor located? Why is favor needed? When favor shows up, can it be recognized? And, can favor be embraced and protected?

In order to unlock favor, it is necessary to pay attention to, then verbally acknowledge, all the small favors God sends. Favor can be as small as finding a close parking space in a crowded lot. When this happens, take a moment to give God thanks. Make thanksgiving a conscience effort, God responds to the one who acknowledges even His smaller blessings.

There are times God will extend favor through the generosity of others. Many times, I have had the honor of being blessed by those who purchased needed, or wanted, items from department stores. And, people have approached me in restaurants in order to pay my bill. When people extend generosity, it is evidence of God's favor and should be received with joy and thanksgiving; without comments like, *"you didn't have to do that,"* *"We are capable of paying for it,"* or *"We are not worthy."* Understand,
God qualified you for favor. How that moment is treated can unlock a greater season, approaching, on the horizon.

I am often asked, *"Can favor increase in my life?"* Of course, my answer is always, *"Absolutely!"*

Luke 2:52 states, *"Jesus grew in wisdom, stature and favor with God and with man."* This is a key to Favor! The willingness to grow will always increase your stature, or influence. Jesus, the Son of God, needed to grow in wisdom in order to know what to do in every situation. His influence increased as his wisdom increased. And, for Jesus' influence to have an impact, He needed to grow in favor with God, and man. So, if the Son of Man required favor for a successful ministry, then favor is necessary for His disciples and followers as well. Favor is God's divine touch upon mankind. It is His supernatural ether, or cloud, that surrounds true believers. And, as the atmosphere begins to thicken, with His presence, He begins to show favor to His people; this cloud is the **FOG**, or Favor of God.

*Favor is that unexplainable promotion, timing, or event that propels you to the next season.*

It is a touch, or season, where it seems you can do no wrong. As a result, people recognize you have been favored by God. A major key to unlocking this divine phenomenon is knowing that the FOG is upon you.

Favor is not automatic, there are qualifications. There is a fundamental understanding necessary in order to move through the Kingdom of God; He doesn't love, He is Love! Love is not earned, nor are we to live for love. If God were a God that showed love, then, He would be led by emotions. However, this is not the case. God Is Love! And, in the Kingdom of God, knowing that God doesn't love, but is Love, is a powerful concept. All His mercies, and all His powerful characteristics, come from what God is, Love. It is important to know, from the beginning, you are LOVED!

What are we living for if not for God's love? His Favor! With God's favor, everything begins lining up with His ordained plan and our lives become a tower of influence for the Kingdom of God. The purpose of favor, His and man's, is to advance the Kingdom of God through healing the sick, raising the dead, cleansing the lepers, and casting out demons.

# 31 Favored Decisions

# 28

# THE WOUND YOU DECIDE TO HEAL

---

*"Wounded People Leak Issues. Wounded people Hurt People, however, Healed People Help People."*
Dr. Jerry Grillo

Emotional wounds, of the past, are common in every individual on earth. One person will, unconsciously, stay anchored to their wound, thereby, causing forward momentum to stop. Another will choose healing in order to move forward in their destiny. Either way, those wounds will create a womb, of a prosperous calling or destiny, filled with failure.

People either accept, or reject, the way other people treat them. However, until past wounds are healed, they will continue to bleed. Many times, they are bandaged with things such as food, alcohol, drugs, work, cigarettes, or sex. Eventually, though, the wounds will begin to ooze and stain everything they touch. At some point, the wounds, and the pain, that bind people to their past, must be addressed; they must make peace with those memories. And, it is imperative to stop giving past emotions the power, or voice, to control our today. Allow yourself to hear the Lord calling you out of yesterday's pain in order to enter His pastures overflowing with healing and power.

Healing for emotional wounds is, ultimately, a decision people must make. Being cut, by a knife, hurts, however, the human body knows exactly how to heal itself. It immediately responds by allowing blood to clot, at the site of the wound, for the purpose of stopping the bleeding. The blood carries white blood cells, along with antibodies, in order to fight the intruders that may have entered the wounded area. Then, a scab is formed over the wound, protects it, and allows healing to take place. After a period of time, the skin is renewed, and a scar forms finishing the healing process. This is the same approach necessary for emotional healing. The bleeding must stop!

## Overcoming the Past

- Recognize that God will never consult your past to discuss your future.
- Don't ignore your past, learn from it. And, never live in your past.
- Live in the now! Looking forward can become overwhelming, so it is important to take baby steps every day.
- Face the wound! Being unwilling to face a wound is a major problem; over time, avoidance makes the wound worse. Don't be afraid to look at it in order to discover the source. Even though there is

pain, it must be healed.
- Forgiveness is vital. Forgiveness is about living, not necessarily about what you, or others, have done. Make an attempt to forgive life for the things that have happened.
- Get over the wound! Face the feelings and get over them.
- Don't allow breakdown moments stop forward momentum. It is easy to quit, but hard to stay the course. However, finishing is a must in order to win.
- If you don't finish the course, what was the point?

You've got this! You have control over your life, no one else. You decide how to respond. The wound is healing!

# 31 Favored Decisions

# 29

# THE PEACE YOU DECIDE TO LIVE IN

What is peace worth to you? My mentor asked this question when we were discussing an issue in my life. Well, actually, I was complaining. After hearing the question, I asked, *"What do you mean?"* He stated, *"Every person needs to have peace."*

## What is peace? Why is it needed? Is peace possible?

Peace is the absence of inner conflict, or the freedom from inner disturbance. Peace is a place absent of warfare. All people have a need for peace; a place without internal war, or external conflicts. Peace is having harmony within and without. It is a state of mind that is not automatic, it comes from a decision. Peace is not a feeling, however, when our focus is on peace, it greatly influences our emotions.

Focusing on the injustices of the past is one of the greatest killers of peace. The unfair treatment of yesterday interrupts the peace available for today. And, without peace, the mind cannot rest, nor is it able to reboot. Sleep, rest, creativity, and meaningful relationships are difficult without peace. The result of lacking peace is a restless mind that is in conflict.

## The absence of peace is RESTLESSNESS.

**Restlessness can be caused by:**

- Fear
- Worry
- Anger
- Unforgiveness
- Bitterness
- Strife
- Pride

Allowing any of these to stay can cause our minds to become fragmented; it is hard to find a worse mental place.

Walking in peace is very important because you get to decide your personal climate. In your surroundings, you can choose what you listen to, then, decide how to respond. You are in position to decide whether, or not, to engage in unwanted conversations which can cause diminished peace. Unfortunately, in most cases, restless people are only attempting to provoke reactions rather than maintaining peace.

## KEYS TO CREATING A PEACEFUL MIND

- *Arguing and conflict can be a trap.* Satan will use moments of conflict in order to frustrate people which can prevent them from finishing the task at hand. Most people have been in arguments and then, after the shouting, realized the fight was over something trivial. It is important to understand what peace is worth so that conflict can be avoided.

- *No one can make you!* Deciding to argue is a choice, no one else can control whether, or not, we enter conflict. The devil can't make people argue, neither can a friend, nor can God.

- *Your focus is creating your feelings.* A person's focus can cause either a response, or a reaction. If a stay-at-home wife, consistently, focuses her husband's absence, angry feelings of abandonment, or the lack of love, could rise to the surface. These emotions can cause restlessness, lack of productivity and, turmoil instead of peace. Yet, he could be taking extra work hours in order to prepare for a surprise, romantic, weekend. However, without her knowing his plan, she is ready to argue when he returns home from work; her face tells the whole story. In this moment of impending conflict, a decision for peace must be made. He can disarm her with the truth.

- *Your reaction is costing you peace.* This statement is self-explanatory. There is no need to say anything else because I want you to have peace.

121

- ***Pay any price to protect your peace.*** I mean it!

- *Pay any price to maintain focus.*

# 30

# THE INVITATION YOU DECIDE TO GIVE

◆━━━━━━━━━━━━━━━━━━━━━━━◆

Not every invitation is a good invitation, and
not every invitation is the right invitation.

In a season, when people desire to be accepted, there's a
real problem of being blinded by an invitation.

An invitation is more powerful than understood. When an
invitation is extended, permission has been granted for
entrance; the notion of belonging has been established. On
Netflix, I watched a movie about Dracula -- Please don't
judge. In the movie, Dracula was standing at the door's
threshold, desperately, wanting to attack the people in the
room. However, he was not able to enter because the
property did not belong to him. Due to the people
recognizing him, they began to shout, "Don't invite him
in!" Prior to this command, Dracula was responding to an
earlier invitation and had partially crossed the threshold;
however, he stopped as the invitation was retracked. Then,
as though with an invisible hand, he was shoved
backwards from the force created by the words, "Don't

invite him in."

How many times have we made wrong decisions by giving invitations to things, or people, that shouldn't have been given?

- Invitation is powerful for protecting your property.
- Invitation connects partners to a vision.
- Invitation is an open door.
- Invitation is never to be trivialized.

Invitation is the key, and power, to an open door; it gives purpose for entry. Invitation can radically change the people surrounding a vision. It is very important to extensively qualify those invited into your life, otherwise, attacks could occur. Dracula, though a fictional story, implies an entry with devastating implications. Remember, if you don't invite it in, it has no right to be there. How much suffering has taken place because we invited the wrong people in?

- Relationships begin with an invitation.
- A smile is an invitation for friendship.
- A handshake is the invitation of agreement.
- A wave is the invitation that you've been noticed.
- Fear is the invitation for mental worry and control.
- Love is an invitation for covenant.
- Hurrying is the invitation for error.
- Giving is the invitation for reaping.

Think how many opportunities have yet to arrive because an invitation wasn't given. Invitations, for others, to join your vision are necessary for growth to occur in your life, business, and ministry.

Salvation is God's invitation to walk with Him.

# 31 Favored Decisions

# 31

# THE SEED YOU
# DECIDE TO SOW

Genesis 8:22
Ecclesiastes 5:3,9
1 Kings 3:3-14
Matthew 26:7-13

One of the most dangerous words, in the bible, is "Seed." In Genesis, chapter two, God made the seed. Though small, the seed represented God's voice which produced great results. They are the fundamental make up, or foundation, of all living things.

The **RIGHT SEED** always gets God's attention. It is important to ask yourself, "What is the right seed?" The right seed is transitional in that it is planted between the gaps of seasons.

## The Seed

- Gains God's attention
- Attracts satanic warfare

- Links you to a man of God
- Authorizes divine promotion
- Unlocks a new season
- Requires uncommon obedience
- Is a portrait of your faith

There are three requirements for sowing the right seed.

- ***You must recognize, and discern, fertile soil.*** In order to have a healthy harvest, it is important to understand you cannot flippantly sow a seed. It must be sown in the proper soil, unlike concrete, or asphalt. However, beneath those surfaces, in the right soil, it can bust through and produce a harvest. By sowing seed into the heart's of people, you can know what kind of soil they are by the harvest it produces. ***"The seed will always reveal the soil."*** However, if the seed is not available to sow, then monitor the soil. When the soil proves worthy, then release the seed.

- ***You must recognize the right season.*** In Genesis, God made the seed before He made the seasons. Thus, He revealed that seasons were created for the seed. And, through seasons, we understand when to sow.

- ***You must discern the right timing.*** Timing is everything; it is the formula that must be unlocked. Wisdom decides the level of God's favor, and favor changes seasons. **Faith decides divine timing**. Timing, and time, are not the same. People don't live in timing, only in time. Looking at the clock tells you what time it is, but time is the moment in which you live, and exist. It is possible to live, in time, while planning for timing. But when you arrive in your tomorrow, which is timing, you will only know time. Time is where people live, but God exists outside of the laws of time. He is always moving in your timing. So, when you sow in the right time, or the right season, and you sow in faith built on expectation, then you activate timing which accelerates back to you in time.

Never trivialize an on-time seed; never ignore an on-time Word; and, never disobey an on-time instruction.

## Facts About Your Seed

- *Your seed must be in a God-directed moment.* For this to be activated, you must develop a sensitivity to God's voice. God will direct you in what you are to sow for His desired harvest.

- *Your seed must be proportionate to your harvest, or dream.* Remember, faith requires a picture. Your seed is the portrait of your faith.

- *Your seed must be important to you.* Sowing an unwanted, or diseased, seed won't bring the desired harvest. And, God will never ask for something you don't have; however, He will ask for those things that are hard to let go of.

- ***Your seed will require the use of faith.*** I mean all of your faith! With faith, you can do just about anything; such as enduring, or exiting, your present situation. With God on your side, faith in your heart, and an ear for His voice, you can do anything. Faith enables you to be, or have, anything within the realm of a seed.

The decision to sow a seed determines how you leave the present, and how you enter the future. With a dream, and a seed, your mind enables you to create a path for its fulfillment.

# CONCLUSION:

How important is a decision? Decisions are made from the moment we awaken to a new day until we shut them again at bedtime; and, they are continually made throughout the day. People decide when to get out of bed and when it is bedtime. Thousands, if not millions, of decisions are made each day. A person's whole life is made up of decisions. Much of what defines a person's life comes as the result of multitudes of yesterday's decisions.

Every good, and bad, relationship, was founded upon a decision. Choices determine the clothes worn, the attitude expressed, even whether to take on new projects. A decision determines the spouse married, the car driven, as well as the home purchased. Life is an accumulation of all the choices made in a lifetime. The good news, if bad decisions were made along the way, there is always an opportunity to make better ones.

I hope this book, "31 Favored Decisions," has been a blessing. I pray you can see how much control you, actually, have over your own life. No one made us who we are, or placed us where we've been. Life's decisions, along with the influence of culture, help to form every individual. However, in reality, the course of our lives depends almost entirely on us. We decide what we can have. We determine what we can do, where we will go, along with what we will become.

## NO ONE HAS POWER OVER YOU!

When someone gains control over another, it is due to

intimidation; they allowed that person to have control. It's my prayer that you make Jesus the Lord of your life. That you will forgive your wrong decisions, study God's word, and allow the Holy Spirit to help you make better choices. May all today's decisions make every tomorrow swim in God's favor.

END NOTES

All definitions were taken ©1995 Zane Publishing, Inc.
©1994, 1991, 1988 Simon & Schuster, Inc.

Made in the USA
Columbia, SC
24 January 2022